BONKERS CLOCKS

Also by Nicholas Fisk from Viking Kestrel

Antigrav

On the Flip Side

A Rag, a Bone and a Hank of Hair

Space Hostages

Sweets from a Stranger and other SF stories

Trillions

You Remember Me!

Nicholas Fisk

BONKERS CLOCKS

Illustrated by Colin West

VIKING KESTREL

VIKING KESTREL

Penguin Books Ltd, Harmondsworth, Middlesex, England
Viking Penguin Inc., 40 West 23rd Street, New York, New York 10010, U.S.A.
Penguin Books Australia Ltd, Ringwood, Victoria, Australia
Penguin Books Canada Ltd, 2801 John Street, Markham, Ontario, Canada L3R 1B4
Penguin Books (N.Z.) Ltd, 182–190 Wairau Road, Auckland 10, New Zealand

First published 1985

Text copyright © Nicholas Fisk, 1985

Illustrations copyright © Colin West, 1985

British Library Cataloguing in Publication Data

Fisk, Nicholas
  Bonkers clocks.
  Rn: David Lee Higginbottom   I. Title
  II. West, Colin
  823'.914[J]   PZ7

ISBN 0-670-80694-3

Typeset, printed and bound in Great Britain by
Hazell Watson & Viney Limited,
Member of the BPCC Group,
Aylesbury, Bucks

That Sunday morning, just when the toast was getting brown, every clock in every house went bonkers.

At the south end of the village where the church is, and the Dying Duck, and the Rumbolds' house, Jenny Rumbold said to her brother Dicko, 'Look!'

'Look at what?'

'Look at the clock! The clock on the mantelpiece!'

'Your toast is ready.' He gave her the piece with the burn on it but she did not even notice. 'Look at the clock!' she repeated.

Dicko looked. The big hand was moving slowly but too fast. It was going like a second hand. '9.35, 9.36, 9.37, 9.38!' it said, in the time it takes to read those numbers. Even as Dicko and Jenny watched, the hand went faster still.

Dicko said, 'I'll show Stanley.' He ran into the hall

to get Stanley, the fat cat. Stanley liked the clock. He usually sat on the mantelpiece staring at it, one half of his furry body bulging over the edge of the shelf. When the clock went 'Ding!', which it did every hour, Stanley blinked, squinted and sniffed at the clock. Sometimes he even touched it with his paw, but generally he was too lazy.

'Look!' Dicko told Stanley, but the cat just tried to yawn. It couldn't yawn properly because its jaw was caught in the crook of Dicko's arm. So Stanley twitched the tip of his tail instead and closed his eyes.

Jenny said, 'I told you he wouldn't be interested.' She was nine, Dicko was ten and Stanley was some-where between the two. The clock had by now worked up a fair old speed. It was on its fourth or fifth trip round the dial and still accelerating. Just as Mum came in, it went 'Ding!' and Dicko said, 'Look Mum! The clock's gone bonkers!'

'You've been messing about with it,' she said. 'Wait till your father finds out . . .'

'I never touched it! Did I, Jen?'

'No, he never touched it. It did it all by itself.'

Dicko said, 'If it goes rushing forward like that, I suppose it *means* something. I suppose it means I'm getting older by the minute.' He began to giggle. His mother said, 'You'll laugh on the other side of your face when your father finds out!' and stared at the clock, worried.

By now, the big hand was a blur and the hour hand, the small hand, was doing an hour every few seconds. The bell went 'Ding . . . Ding . . . Ding', and Stanley was squinting in time with it. He even stretched out his fat paw, but thought better of it and blinked and squinted instead.

'Older by the minute,' Dicko repeated. 'I'll be an old man with a white beard any moment now!'

But his mother said, 'No you won't.' She had her nose right against the clock's glass. 'You'll get younger,' she said. 'It's going backwards.'

'Forwards!' said Jenny, putting her face by her mother's to peer at the clock.

'Backwards. Look at the hour hand. Eleven, ten, nine, eight –'

'Forwards, Mum! It's going five, six, seven, eight –'

'Don't contradict,' Mum said, still worried. 'Eat your breakfast.'

Dad came in and Mum said, 'The clock's gone wrong, Arthur.'

Dad looked at the clock (it was whizzing away like mad) and turned to Dicko. 'Now then, Dicko,' he said grimly, 'what did you do to the clock?'

'I never –!' Dicko said.

'He never –!' Jenny said. Even Stanley looked coldly at Mr Rumbold, as if to say, 'Fancy accusing your own son! Tsk, Tsk!'

So Mr Rumbold gave up, and looked at the clock. It was going faster than ever. 'I've never heard of a clock going *backwards*,' he said.

'Forwards,' said Dicko and Jenny.

'Backwards,' said Mr Rumbold. 'I am looking at it and it's going backwards. Isn't it, Madge?'

But Mrs Rumbold wasn't listening. The clock was now breaking all records for speed. Dicko had stopped giggling – he was busy with toast and marmalade – but Jenny had caught the giggles from him. 'Time flies!' she said, between her tee-hees and snufflings. She nudged Dicko to make sure he got the joke. Mr Rumbold said, 'Jenny, eat your breakfast.'

'It's not breakfast, it's the day after tomorrow's dinner by now!' Dicko told Jenny, under his breath. He grinned, she giggled. Their father looked at them disgustedly and said, 'There's no peace in this house.'

From the hall, their mother said, 'Arthur! The big clock out here is doing it too! Going like – like – clockwork . . .'

Mr Rumbold just grunted and buttered his toast.

Later on that Sunday morning, Dicko fed Stanley; Jenny did some homework to get it over and done with so that she could watch TV that evening; their father worked in the garden; and Mrs Rumbold made the evening dinner.

Other people went to church, cleaned cars, made beds, prepared lunches, served petrol in garages and sweets in the sweetshop, exercised ponies, tinkered with motorbikes – they did a thousand things because

8

there were about a thousand people in the village. Some of them, of course, talked about the clocks going mad.

And all the time, the clocks continued to go bonkers.

All the children said they were going forwards.

All the adults said they were going backwards.

Exactly at noon, every single clock and watch behaved itself again and told the right time.

But by then – *it had happened*.

We must go back half an hour, to 11.30 in the morning.

At that time, Madge Rumbold called out to her husband – who had not finished motor-mowing the lawn – 'Arthur! You'll have to stop that and come in and get changed! We're going ·to Miss Lofting's, remember?'

So Mr Rumbold reluctantly stopped the mower and went inside to wash, put on a suit and tie and make himself respectable.

He did this because Miss Lofting was in charge of the local school; once a year she held a party – a 'Sunday get-together' – for teachers and parents. It was an important occasion, because Miss Lofting was a firm-minded lady. Her roses never had mildew or greenfly, they were not allowed to. When she called her little dog, a King Charles Spaniel named Roderigo, it looked more than ever as if it had just been shot – its pop-eyes almost popped out of its head and it did not merely walk, but ran to obey its mistress.

Mr Rumbold therefore changed his clothes. Mrs Rumbold straightened his tie. The party began at 12.45, which meant twelve forty-five precisely. When they were ready and Madge Rumbold had quite finished patting her hair in front of the mirror, they went downstairs. Dicko and Jenny were waiting for them.

'We're going now,' said Mrs Rumbold.

Now, that was a very ordinary thing to say, but Mrs Rumbold did not say it in the ordinary way. She did not sound much like a mother talking to her children. Her voice seemed to have changed: to have become nervous, high-pitched, almost childish.

'We're going now,' she said again. Jenny did not answer. Dicko just frowned. Mrs Rumbold giggled and Mr Rumbold started to whistle between his teeth, very softly.

At last, Jenny said, 'Let's have a look at your hands, then. Both of you.'

Obediently, Mr and Mrs Rumbold held out their hands for inspection. Jenny took hold of her father's hands, turned them over and looked closely at the nails. 'That won't do,' she said, grimly. 'Upstairs and scrub those nails!'

'But I did!' her father replied, wide-eyed. 'I did scrub them! With the brush! Honest!'

Jenny said, 'You've got enough of the garden in those nails to grow a pound of Brussels sprouts. No arguments. Up, up, up, up, UP!'

And humbly, Mr Rumbold crept up the stairs to the bathroom.

'*My* hands are clean!' Mrs Rumbold said, smirking and simpering. Dicko gave her a stern look and said, 'Your brooch is all crooked . . . That's better.'

Mr Rumbold came downstairs and silently and sulkily held out his hands. Jenny gave a long sigh, rolled her eyes heavenwards and said, 'Well, I suppose that will have to do. Off with you, then! And be careful on the roads, do you hear?'

Mr and Mrs Rumbold, relieved, scuttled away. Dicko and Jenny heard the car being started. 'Ought to walk,' Dicko grumbled. 'Use the car for everything. What's wrong with their legs, I'd like to know? Bone idle. Where's the newspaper?'

Mr Rumbold drove the car past the front of the house. It was his new car, a Vauxhall. Mrs Rumbold, sitting beside him, waved shyly as the car went by.

Jenny said, 'Well! That's *them* out of the way for an hour or so! I'll have to get on, I suppose . . .' She began plumping up the cushions on the sofa in the living-room and straightening things on the mantel-piece, shaking her head whenever she found some-thing out of place.

Dicko said, 'Peace at last, eh? Think I'll have a chat with Stanley. Come on, old chap!' He put the cat under one arm, the newspaper under the other, and went to his bedroom. He said, as he settled himself in front of the newspaper, 'Don't know what the coun-try's coming to, Stanley, I really don't. Blasted poli-ticians!'

He went on and on about politicians, getting quite red in the face.

Stanley slept.

A lot of people were already at Miss Lofting's house when Mr and Mrs Rumbold arrived.

Miss Lofting was standing by her garden gate welcoming her guests. 'Such a lovely day!' she said. 'Aren't we fortunate? Yes, the roses *are* wonderful this year, aren't they?'

Under her breath, she added, 'And they're all mine and you can't have any.'

Mr Rumbold got out of his car smiling. It was a

bright red Vauxhall with a gold stripe along the side. He was proud of it. He began to say, 'Well, hallo Miss Lofting!' – but never finished. For Mr Finching, the Bank Manager, was sitting in his car with both hands pressing down the horn button. Mrs Finching was hitting him with her handbag to try and stop him, but he took no notice. He just chuckled and the horn went BLAH BLAH BLAAH.

Mr Rumbold's smile faded. He stuck out his lower lip, went back to his car, sat down in it and made the horn play WE ARE THE CHAMPIONS, BLAH-BLAH, BLA-A-AH.

The women all clustered together, pursing their lips, rolling their eyes and chattering. They said, 'Aren't men *stupid*, they're so *stupid*! They spoil *everything*!' and nodded at each other until their hats almost fell off.

Mr Finching and Mr Rumbold suddenly got tired of horn-blowing and got out of their cars. Mr Finching said, 'What's that supposed to be then?' and pointed rudely at Mr Rumbold's new Vauxhall.

'It's my Vauxhall. My new Vauxhall!' said Mr Rumbold, looking the Bank Manager straight in the eye.

'New, is it?' said Mr Finching, nastily. 'Wonder where you got the money? Wonder who lent you the money? Bet I know. Bet I could tell!'

'You better not,' said Mr Rumbold, grimly. 'You just better not, see? You just better keep your fat mouth shut, that's all – *moneybags*!'

But Mr Finching was grinning and pretending not to hear. '*My* car's not a Vauxhall,' he said. 'Mine's a Jaguar. Jaguar, Jaguar, Jaguar!'

'Who cares?' shouted Mr Rumbold. 'Who cares about your car? Who cares about a rotten old Jaguar? It's not new, like mine! Mine's got new paint, new engine, new everything! New all through! Yours is old and rotten and grotty!'

But now Mr Finching had thought of a new way to annoy Mr Rumbold. He pushed his fingernail into the red paint of Mr Rumbold's car. The nail made a squeaky noise against the shine. 'Squeaky clean!' he sang in a high squeaky voice. 'Someone's car is squeaky clean!'

'You take your hands off my car.'

'Won't. Squeaky clean, squeaky clean –'

'You jolly well will!'

'I jolly well won't!'

They began to fight, rolling about on the ground beside the two cars. The women drew away, sniffing

with disgust. 'There's men for you!' they told each
other. 'Tsk! Tsk!'

The two men got tired of fighting and stood up to
dust each other down. Mr Finching said, 'I could have
karate-chopped you just then. WHAM. But I'd have
broken your arm. Right off. Just like that, one karate
chop!' He picked bits of grass off Mr Rumbold's suit
and continued, 'It's not bad, your new car. I like red
for a car and that's a super red.'

'I like Jaguars best,' said Mr Rumbold. He too was
tired of fighting and wanted to be friends. '*Varoom*!
M-yeah, m-yeah! They're great, Jaguars. But then,
my Vauxhall is new and your Jaguar's old, so I don't
know which I like best.'

'What about a Ferrari, then?' said Mr Finching.

'Hundred and sixty miles an hour! A *red* Ferrari! *Vroom-vroom! Va-rang-ang-ang!*'

They began running in the front garden between the roses, faster and faster, pretending to be red Ferraris.

The rest of the guests were in Miss Lofting's little house. Miss Lofting herself was pouring drinks for them. She had whisky, gin, sherry, tonic water, dry ginger and soda water. There were lemon slices, ice, salt biscuits, olives and peanuts in small saucers for those who cared to take them. She had prepared everything very well.

She said to Mrs Rumbold, 'Madge, my dear – I may call you Madge, mayn't I, on an occasion like this – what will you have?'

'Oh – my usual gin and tonic, that would be lovely. Thank you so much. And yes, a slice of lemon. Lovely.'

Miss Lofting served all her other guests, raised her own glass and said, in the loud, clear voice she used to bring classes to order, 'May I have your attention for just a moment . . . yes, thank you so much, just for a moment . . . May I just say my usual word of welcome to you all? Welcome! And shall we drink a wee toast to another happy and successful school year, which already promises to be –'

But Mr Blanchflower the butcher (whose son Fred went to the school) had tasted his drink – taken a good pull of it, filled his mouth with it: and before Miss Lofting could finish her speech, there was a loud '*Ptoo!*' as Mr Blanchflower, face twisted, spat his drink on the carpet!

'Eeeuck!' he gasped. 'It's awful! Ghastly! Horrible! Like acid!'

When the shock of Mr Blanchflower's behaviour was over, the other guests sipped carefully at their drinks. They too made faces.

'Yuck!' they said.
'Bitter!'
'Foul!'
'Burns my throat!'
Miss Lofting, completely puzzled, tasted her own

drink – her usual dry sherry. She rolled the drink over her tongue. Her face twisted. She cried, 'Ooo! Foul! Sour! Acid!' She sniffed the drink, pulled a face and said, 'And what a *pong!*'

Everyone stared at everyone else, hopelessly embarrassed. Miss Lofting was the first to recover. 'Come on, everyone!' she said, 'Follow me! Into the kitchen! I've got two great big bottles somewhere, bottles I keep for the children . . .' She rooted about in a cupboard and then, triumphant, held up two bottles. 'Yes! Here they are! One lemon squash, one orange squash!'

'Sooper-de-luxe!' someone shouted, and after that, with proper, sweet drinks for everyone, the party went very well; except for a few fights on the carpet when the men got over-excited.

Mrs Rumbold, who was tucking peanuts into the top of her bra for when she got home, said to her husband Arthur, 'Well, I think it's a jolly good party but I wish you'd stop fighting. I mean, really . . .'

He said, 'It wasn't fighting, not really fighting. If it had been a real fight I'd have duffed him up proper with my Bionic Bash! I'd have –'

'Oh, do *stop* it, Arthur.' Trying to change the subject and make him forget about fighting and Bionic Bashes, she said, 'Where are the Patels?'

'The Patels?' said Mr Rumbold.

'You know. That woman, that Indian woman, with the Indian husband and the two children. Indian children. The Patels!'

'Oh, I don't know,' said Mr Rumbold. 'Look, I've got some peanuts in my trousers pocket. Let's swipe some biscuits –'

'Don't change the subject!' his wife said. 'Why aren't they here? Their children go to the school, so why aren't they here? Why isn't *she* here? Mrs Patel? She *ought* to be here. She's a new parent, they've only just moved in, it's her *duty* to be here.'

Mr Rumbold now remembered the Patels. He had waved his hand and said 'Hallo' to Mr Patel, who was a serious but pleasant-looking man of about his own age. The children were dark-eyed and quiet. Mrs Patel was very pretty; and a strange person to see in an English village, because her hair was dark and long and her dresses were bright and long. Walking along the high street or doing her shopping, she seemed like a Bird of Paradise among sparrows. He had never spoken to her.

'She *ought* to be here,' his wife said.

'What a swiz, all the crisps are gone,' Mr Rumbold replied.

'If she were here,' Madge Rumbold said – determined not to be put off course – 'you'd be all over her!' Her face had gone hard and mean. 'Saris with gold edges,' she continued. 'Making a parade of herself in those clothes! Too stuck-up to come, that's why she's not here!'

'If she did come, you'd only be rude to her,' said Mr Rumbold, puzzled.

'Jolly well serve her right,' said Madge.

Mr Rumbold turned away from his wife and talked to Mr Ramsey, the insurance man. He said to Mr Ramsey, 'My wife's going on about Mrs Patel. Saying nasty things.'

Mr Ramsey said, 'Oh, they're all right. The Patels, I mean. He's got that little grocery shop. He works like anything. Open all hours. He ought to insure it, but he won't. He's trying to get an allotment, we were talking about it the other day –'

Mrs Ramsey joined the conversation. There was a spiteful look on her face, like the look on Mrs Rumbold's. She said, 'Well, I must say! So that's where you spend your time, talking to Mrs Patel!'

Her husband said, 'It was *Mister* Patel. We were talking about allotments –'

'Flouncing around in long silk dresses,' Mrs Ramsey interrupted. 'A fine thing it would be if I was to behave like that. Or Madge. Silk dresses with gold edges –'

Mr Finching said, 'Perhaps I shouldn't say this, but I happen to know – being a Bank Manager and going into people's homes and talking money with them – I happen to know that the Patels aren't exactly *rich*. Perhaps they don't want to spend money on clothes. Or perhaps she just prefers wearing Indian clothes. They look nicer. I think so, anyhow.'

'Oh!' said his wife, raising her eyebrows very high and making her mouth completely circular, 'So that's it! You've been going into the Patels' home! Into that woman's home! Having little chats with her, no doubt! Admiring her silk dresses with gold edges!'

'Have an olive,' Mr Finching said, trying to stuff his wife's mouth with one so that she couldn't talk any

more. He actually got the olive in, but she spat it out again, very hard – so hard that it went right across the room and bounced off the wall.

Someone said, 'Soooper!' and someone else said, 'Brill!' and soon people were cramming olives into their mouths and trying to fire them out again, like bullets. There were plenty of olives left, of course. Since the clocks had gone mad, nobody liked the taste of bitter or acid things. But the olives made good bullets, so they put up with the salty taste.

Even Miss Lofting (who was shocked when an olive hit her on the back of her head) got into the spirit of the thing after a time, but she wasn't very good at it. Her olives only went *Pop* and travelled a few feet. Some of the grown-ups could fire them with amazing power and a noise like an air-rifle going off.

Not everyone was firing olives. Mr Scrivener wasn't. He owned the tool-hire shop. He was a foxy man, not tall, who wore patterned shirts with ties having a quite different pattern. He was sharp-looking. Recently, his business had not been going very well so he felt anxious and cross. He felt someone ought to be to blame.

In the middle of the olive-popping, Mr Scrivener's voice said, loud and clear, 'You know what? They're making charlies out of us! That's what they're doing, making charlies!'

Mr Finching the Bank Manager said, 'What? Who's making charlies out of us?'

'All those Patels,' Mr Scrivener said, scowling. 'They come over here and start businesses and take the bread out of our mouths. The *bread*,' he repeated, 'out of our *mouths*.'

On the other side of the room, Mr Smith the librarian fired off a particularly loud and successful olive, but no one paid any attention. They were too busy listening to Mr Scrivener, who was nodding his foxy head slowly. 'Taking the bread out of our *children's* mouths!' he said.

Mrs Rumbold, wide-eyed, said, 'The Patels don't really do that, do they?' She was seeing, in her mind's eye, her own children, Dicko and Jenny: both with bread in their mouths. Then along come the Patels, and – no more bread! Just open mouths! 'I don't believe the Patels would do that,' she murmured.

Miss Lofting said, 'Of course they don't! What nonsense! How stupid to say such a thing!'

But Mrs Ramsey, wildly excited, jumped up on the sofa, waved her arms and shouted, 'Oh yes they do! And if you men were really men, you'd get rid of them! But that's the trouble, you're not real men, you're just blobby little rotten weaklings!' She waved her arms still harder, then began to cry.

This upset the women, who tried to comfort Mrs Ramsey; and stirred up the men. They turned to Mr Scrivener, waiting for a lead.

Mr Scrivener made his eyes go narrow and dangerous. His head sank into his shoulders. His voice changed. He said, 'Wanna know what I think? We oughta run them coyotes outta town onna rail! Hanging's too good for them coyotes!' He looked and sounded just like Mutt Wildblood in that TV series about the Wild West (you know the one).

Many of the women looked at Mr Scrivener with a new admiration in their eyes. So did some of the men. Mr Blanchflower narrowed his eyes and spoke. He said, 'I gotta rod. And it's loaded. Get me, pardner?' He winked at Mr Scrivener, who winked back and nodded.

Mr Rumbold was not happy about all this. He said, 'Wait a minute, just wait a sec, oughtn't we –' But nobody listened to him. Instead, they watched Mr Blanchflower as he strode from the room. 'Gonna get me my rod,' he said grimly.

He lived only two houses away and soon returned with his gun. He really did have one. It was a Webley revolver from World War II. Or most of it, anyhow: only the trigger and the revolving bit that holds cartridges were missing. 'Mah shootin' iron!' he said. The men crowded around to admire it.

Within minutes, the air was loud with the sound of car engines as the men roared off to their homes to get weapons.

While all this was happening at Miss Lofting's, Jenny and Dicko had been busy at home.

Jenny soon finished her work. She left the washing-up and other difficult bits, but made sure all the cushions were plumped up again, switched the vacuum cleaner on and off, straightened rugs, folded news-papers and readjusted some flowers from the garden in their vase. As she worked she said, 'Tsk, tsk!' or 'Really . . .!', or 'I'll *never* get done!'

When she came across her school books, she pulled a face. Housework was over: she had to do her homework.

When she sat down at her little desk and opened the books, a horrible shock awaited her. The book said:

Exercise: Tesselation Sheet
1. Label the angles of one triangle, X Y and Z as shown, and cut out the shape.
2. Using this triangle, mark on the tesselation sheet other angles with the same measurement as:
a) <X b) <Y c) <Z

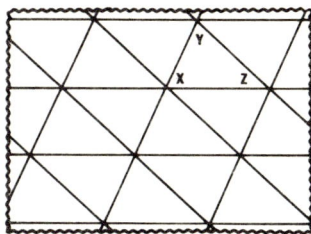

Jenny knew this ought to make sense to her, but it did not. It was as if she were seeing a ghost from another time, a ghost of something or someone she had once known . . . But now it was all a mystery to her. There was a sort of crisscross grid, like window panes made of diamond-shaped glass; and there was an X and a Y and a Z in the grid.

'Oh dear!' she said and looked through her exercise books. Though they were in her own writing, they meant nothing to her! Nothing at all! She began to panic and went to her brother's room.

Dicko was still in his room lecturing Stanley the cat about politics. When Jenny came in, he looked up gravely from under his brows, folded his paper, laid it aside and said, 'Yes, my dear? What seems to be the trouble?'

'I seem to be in a bit of a mess with this homework,' she said worriedly, fiddling with an end of her hair just as her mother did. 'This tesselation sheet . . .'

'Ah,' Dicko said wisely. 'A tesselation sheet. Yes,

25

indeed.' Jenny could tell that Dicko was just as lost as she was. Stanley the cat provided a distraction. Stanley, ears back and eyes blazing, was being kittenish. He was pouncing on one of Dicko's shoes, pretending to be a tiger. As he was a large, respectable, elderly cat, it did not suit him to be kittenish.

Dicko threw the homework book aside. 'We have graver concerns to discuss, my dear,' he said. 'Matters concerning the whole subject of education. Indeed, I feel obliged to ask myself, "What precisely is the *value* of school?"'

'But Richàrd – !'

'No, do not interrupt me. Stanley, *stop* that. Need there be school, Jennifer? Should there be school? Is it useful? Is it valuable? Stanley, *stop* that. Can a mere school truly prepare us for the tasks we will eventually face in everyday life?'

'Can it?' Jenny gasped, amazed by her brother's daring thoughts.

'My answer must be – NO!' Dicko cried, bringing his hand down on the bed with such a thump that Stanley scampered from the room, tail up and ears right back. 'No, no, NO!' Dicko repeated. 'School is futile! Meaningless! Pointless! In fact, Jenny,' he said, sounding more like his old self, 'school is a load of codswallop!'

'But Richard, children always go to school,' she objected. 'I mean, us . . . the others . . . we'll all be going to school for years yet!'

'No we won't,' Dicko said, firmly.

'But what will we do instead?'

'A hundred things, Jennifer. A thousand. A million. Just think of the things we could do! There's the house, and the garden, and all the other things –'

'What other things?' she said. Like her brother, she was feeling a warm excitement creep over her.

'Well, there's the car, isn't there? I mean, you can't start driving too early. And the lawnmower. I never get a go at the lawnmower – not a proper one. Dad and Mum have all the fun, they run the whole show.'

'But we've got to get an education,' Jenny said, worriedly, 'so that we can earn a living. Get a good job.'

'Who needs education? Who needs a good job? All you need is money!'

'How would we make money?'

'Well, that's obvious! I know all sorts of super jobs I could do! I could use the car to start a taxi service. Or I could put the motor mower in the back of the car and go round cutting everyone's lawn. We'd make pots!'

'And I could become a pop star!' said Jenny. 'And if that didn't work right away, I could make lots of cakes on the new cooker and sell them. I know how to make Quiche Lorraine!'

'Bet I'd make more than you with the lawnmower,' Dicko said. 'And the grass needs cutting right now. Dad didn't finish. I suppose you think I can't work the mower? Bet you I can!'

'And I suppose you think I can't make fantastic puddings and cakes and sweets and things? Because I can!'

'Jennifer,' Dicko said, going back to his pompous manner. 'Actions speak louder than words. Possibly you have some doubts about my ability to use the lawnmower effectively? If so, perhaps a demonstration will convince you.'

'Bet you can't get it to go!' she said.

'I shall first,' said her dignified brother, 'change the trainers I am wearing for stouter, more protective footwear. After that – well, just *watch*!'

He strode from the room. 'I will watch!' Jenny shouted after him. 'And then I'll make a gorgeous pudding, the sort people pay pounds and pounds for!'

She heard the clank and rumble of the motor mower as her brother pulled it out of the shed, over the gravel and on to the lawn. She opened the bedroom window, just over the spot where Dicko was, and leaned out. 'But you don't know how to work it!' she shouted.

In answer, he adjusted the lever to START, pulled the rubber-handled cord – and the engine roared into life.

The men came back to Miss Lofting's house waving guns over their heads.

There was a broken shotgun, a real-looking Mauser that fired water, two airguns (one with a telescopic sight), a revolver that would have fired if the bits hadn't been missing; and a mixed assortment of blunderbusses, fowling pieces and other firearms of the sort that you hang over mantelpieces. None of these fired, of course, but all looked good when waved.

Mr Ramsey had a firearm that really did work. It was a pistol that fired blanks. 'It makes a super bang!' Mr Ramsey said. 'Loud as anything! I bet it's the loudest blank pistol in the whole world!'

Everyone but Miss Lofting was very excited. Mr Inkpen, who ran the garage, was telling a man who owned a blunderbuss how to load it with small ball bearings. Mrs Ramsey was being a Dalek, croaking 'Exterminate! Exterminate!' So was Mrs Ambrose from the cake shop but she did not do it quite so well.

Mr Finching kept loading and unloading his airgun. He pointed it at a collection of small stuffed birds under a glass dome and cried, 'You're dead! Bang!' He pulled the trigger and the birds stared at him with their faded, glassy eyes, looking very dead indeed.

Miss Lofting sat in a corner on the floor with her legs stuck straight out in front of her. She was afraid that someone would break the porcelain figurines she was so proud of. She cried weakly and said, 'You are all silly pigs! Silly pigs!' It was her house and she did not want it spoiled.

And suddenly everyone was being Red Indians. The little house echoed and shook with Indian war-whoops. Faces were flushed, feet trampled in rhythm, guns were waved. Mr Scrivener stood on the sofa and hit a saucepan as if it were a tomtom. Soon all Miss Lofting's guests were circling and dancing round him, making 'Oller-woller-woller' noises, very loudly.

It was Mr Rumbold who brought the meeting to order. He was still puzzled and confused about the Patels. He wanted to say something, but did not know what. So he stood up and shouted, 'Listen to me, everyone! About the Patels –'

Mr Scrivener said, 'That's right, they're taking the bread out of our mouths!' and Mrs Ramsey said, 'No, that's wrong, it's out of the *children's* mouths! They ought to be roasted alive!'

Mr Scrivener wanted everyone to listen to him, so he jumped on the sofa, waved his arms and said, in his special, cowboy-movie voice, 'OK, folks, now just you lissen to me. We don't want no roasting alive, that's not the way we folks do things. That's Injun talk and we ain't no darned Injuns, right?'

'We were a minute ago,' someone said. 'We were all going oller-woller-woller! I *liked* going oller-woller-woller!'

No one wanted to hear this person, however. They wanted Mr Scrivener. He said, 'OK, folks; let's settle down. Hear me real good.' Everyone was silent. 'Know what we're goin' to do, pardners? We're goin' to run those Injuns, those Patels, outta town onna rail! That's what we're gonna do! Yes sirree!'

Most of his audience cheered. But Mr Rumbold objected, 'What's the good of our guns, then? I mean, guns are for *shooting*, not for running folks out of towns on rails.' Several people agreed with him and he smiled.

Mr Scrivener, though, had no intention of losing his audience. 'Sure we're going to shoot them!' he yelled. 'Shoot 'em first, run 'em outta town later! OK?'

'OK!' they replied, waving their guns with new energy.

'So wadda we waiting for?' Mr Scrivener shouted.

'Lunch!' shouted Mr Ramsey. 'I'm starving,' he said. 'Let's all go home and get something to eat, and then come back and shoot the Patels, or someone. But food first, don't you think?'

Everyone agreed. 'Home for lunch!' they cried.

Mr Rumbold said, 'I'm not going *home*, I'm taking my wife to a *pub* for lunch! I've got real money in my pocket, lots and lots of it!' He jingled the money in his pocket. You could tell that he felt very grand having real money to spend in a pub.

Mr Scrivener, pouting because people were not paying attention to him, said, 'OK, folks. Food first, but – you better believe me – after chow, we're gonna gun down those coyotes by the light of the moon. Am I right, or am I right?'

'You're right!' they shouted.

Mr Scrivener nodded his head several times and said, 'At sundown, then, OK? I want you to wear masks and carry lanterns –'

'I haven't got a proper mask,' someone objected.

'A handkerchief will do,' Mr Scrivener said, 'And if you ain't got lanterns, better make it torches. Then we all creep up, masked, in the light of the full moon, and we surround the Patel house – and *pow-wow-wow!* We gun 'em down, showing no mercy! Yippie-i-yay!'

'Yippie-i-yay!' everyone cried. Even Miss Lofting cheered up a little, perhaps because she was hungry and wanted to get at some chocolate biscuits she had hidden in her larder.

So everyone went off in cars with a warm, glowing, expectant feeling inside about what they would do to the Patels when the moon was full and torches flared and guns glinted. 'I can't wait!' Mrs Rumbold told Mr Rumbold, 'At least, I *can* wait because I'm so hungry, but you know what I mean . . .'

'Pow-pow-pow!' murmured Mr Rumbold; and headed his car to the Dying Duck.

The motor mower's engine roared into life when Dicko pulled the starter cord. But then it stopped. He began to swear. Above him, in the window, Jenny's voice giggled.

Stanley's face appeared in the window beside Jenny. The cat looked down at Dicko's back and his tail twitched. Dicko's back seemed, to the kittenish cat, an inviting place.

Dicko bent over and pulled at the starter, again and again. 'Have you got the petrol turned on?' Jenny asked, sweetly. She had guessed, correctly, that he had forgotten about the tap.

Furiously, Dicko bent over the machine so that his body hid whatever he was doing to the petrol tap, and shouted, 'Do you think I'm *stupid* or something?' He bent down to turn the tap on and grasp the starter handle.

His back looked exactly right to Stanley. The cat quivered, twitched its tail, then launched itself out of the window. Just as the mower started, the cat landed, digging in firmly with its claws.

Dicko yelled, 'Ouch!' The mower started and said, 'Roar!' Jenny gasped, giggled and said, 'Ooo!'

Things became complicated. The mower had an automatic clutch: it drove itself. The person behind it was supposed to tell it where to go, but Dicko was too busy. He spun round in circles trying to reach Stanley, who was attached to the seat of his trousers and the flesh of his backside by sharp claws. The more Dicko spun, the less chance Stanley had of pulling in his claws. Neither Dicko nor Stanley was happy with this situation.

The mower, however, seemed quite contented. It chuntered off happily on its own, the motor going better and better as it warmed up. Full of determination and petrol, it bumped over some paving stones; found some gravel to chew and spit out; then a nice

stretch of lawn to cut; and at last, Dicko's training shoes. He had placed them neatly, side by side, on the lawn.

You could tell that the mower enjoyed the trainers. They were a challenge. The canvas uppers and lace holes were easy meat, of course. The rotating blade chewed them up as easily as a dragon chewed a knight without armour.

However, the rubber soles put up quite a fight. They even slowed the engine down. But the mower triumphed in the end – there were bits of rubber bouncing about all over the place. So the mower speeded up and moved on to further triumphs.

It tried to climb a rose bush and eat that too. It could not. It only reached the name label at the bottom. So it gave up, stopped, and was silent.

Stanley had by now released himself from Dicko's back and was making a series of babyish pounces, straight up and down, on a bumblebee. Dicko could have kicked the cat. He contented himself, as he picked up the remains of his trainers, with flinging Stanley in the air by the scruff of the neck. Stanley landed on all fours and, delighted with this new game, came back mewing for more.

Jenny rattled the window catch noisily to let Dicko know that she had observed and enjoyed the whole scene. She sniffed loudly; said, 'Well . . .! I suppose you're satisfied now!' and went to get a late lunch. She decided on tinned spaghetti with bits of sausage in it to be followed by tinned peaches.

35

The tin-opener, always awkward, did not want to grip the tin. She turned the handle faster but all that happened was that bits of paper from the label got caught up in the little toothed wheel that was meant to keep the tin turning.

Outside, she heard the motor mower. Dicko had got it going properly now, and its roarings were rhythmical as he walked up and down. Determined not to be outdone, Jenny wound the tin-opener handle furiously. Grr, grr, grr, went the little toothed wheel, actually getting rid of the bits of paper that had choked it. Jenny smiled.

The tin, having travelled full circle and parted from its lid, released itself from the tin-opener and fell on her foot.

Jenny watched in despair as a particularly juicy sliver of sliced peach slithered oilily into the gap between her foot and shoe. She felt her shoe fill with the sticky liquid.

Stanley appeared. He poked his head at the mess on the floor and dabbed at a peach slice with his paw, hoping it was a goldfish. It wasn't, so he walked away, leaving a line of sticky paw marks.

Lunch was not really a happy meal. Mowing the lawn had proved more tiring than Dicko had expected. The mower seemed to have a mind of its own. Cutting grass seemed to bore it. It would rather stop. When it stopped it was hard to start again.

'Let's have a sherry,' Dicko said. He poured the drinks but the taste was not what either of them expected. They did not finish their glasses but sat in silence, thinking their own thoughts and prodding at the tinned spaghetti and sausage without much appetite. 'I thought this stuff was meant to be heated,' Dicko grumbled.

'I haven't time for everything,' Jenny replied. 'There's the rest of the house to see to,' she continued, thinking of the mess under the tin-opener, still to be cleared up. She moved her right foot. It went 'glug'. Peach juice.

For afters, they had an apple and an orange each. There seemed nothing to say. Only Stanley was at ease. He was asleep on a cushion. Jenny said, 'Things somehow don't feel right. I feel as if something were missing . . . I don't know. And it's school tomorrow.'

'We are not going back to school,' Dicko told her. 'Not ever. All that is past. I thought I'd explained all that, Jennifer.'

'Yes, you did,' she said, miserably. 'And it seemed right at the time. But I don't know . . .' She stopped:

her hand went to her mouth. 'Dicko! I know what's wrong! Mum and Dad! They're not here!'

'Good heavens!' said Dicko, jumping to his feet. 'You're right! What's happened to them? They should have been home hours ago. Did they say they were going somewhere?'

'No! Not a word!'

'Blasted, irresponsible *parents*!' said Dicko, striding about furiously. 'Things were very different when they were *my* age, I can tell you!'

'What do we do? We've got to find them!'

'They can't be far. If only we'd got the car!'

'We've got bicycles. We'll go on our bikes.'

'No. Let's telephone around first.'

Jenny went to the telephone and dialled.

She rang Miss Lofting. She heard the phone lifted and breathing at the other end of the line. Jenny said, 'Hallo. Hallo . . .?'

'Hallo yourself,' Miss Lofting at last replied. Her voice sounded a bit strange. 'This is Miss Lofting. Double hallos and no returns.'

'No, please . . . This is Jenny Rumbold, Miss Lofting. My parents –'

'Silly fat pigs, all of them,' said Miss Lofting.

'Look, Miss Lofting, this is serious. Please listen.

My parents, Mr and Mrs Rumbold, haven't come home –'

'RUM-bold, RUM-bold! Rumble-tummy RUM-bold!' sang Miss Lofting, giggling. There was a click, then silence.

'She hung up,' Jenny said to Dicko. 'Now what do I do?'

'Try the Ramseys,' Dicko suggested.

But the Ramseys were just as bad.

Mrs Ramsey answered the phone. She said, 'Hal-lo-o-o,' just like a little girl giving an imitation of a respectable old lady. Jenny said, 'Please, Mrs Ramsey, this is rather important. This is Jenny Rumbold speaking –'

'I know who you are,' Mrs Ramsey interrupted. 'You're Jenny. Just a titchy little *girl*. I'm a grown-up *lady*, I'm Mrs Ramsey!'

'Yes, I know that, Mrs Ramsey, but please listen –'

Mr Ramsey's voice replaced Mrs Ramsey's. He said, 'Old chairs to mend! Old chairs to mend!'

'Mr Ramsey, I'm trying to find my parents, I need your help –'

But by now, Mr Ramsey was singing a song about a motor-car that went poop, poop, poop, as it went along the road. He sang very loudly. Jenny put the phone down and stared at Dicko. 'What's happening?' she said.

'Whatever it is, it's getting worse. Everything's upside down.'

'At first they behaved like children. That was bad enough. Now they're almost like babies.'

'Is something happening to us, too, do you think?' Dicko asked.

'No! Of course not! At least, I don't think so . . .'

'Well, we've got to find Mum and Dad. That is our first duty.' He looked very solemn. 'Let's get on our bikes. Obviously it is no good telephoning.'

'But where shall we look?'

'We'll try the police station first.'

By now, the afternoon was getting older, whatever the clocks said. The shadows were beginning to lengthen. They got their bikes, mounted them and began their search for the missing parents.

On their way, they rang on doors and went into shops. It seemed that hardly anyone was at home. Sometimes, they knew there were people behind the closed doors because, when they rang bells or knocked knockers, there were sounds of stifled giggling. One young housewife whose name they did not know actually answered the door. They began to ask the usual question – 'Please, have you seen our parents, Mr and Mrs Rumbold' – but the housewife answered, 'Look! I can stand on my head!' And did so.

But then they met three more children: ten-year-old Allie Ramsey, whose real name was Alexandra; Pete Scrivener, nine; and Chris Inkpen, the garageman's youngest son, aged six.

'Listen, you three, you've got to help us!' Jenny said. 'All the parents are going crazy and we've got to stop them before they do some real damage –'

'My parents aren't crazy,' Chris Inkpen said. 'My dad's cleverer than anyone. He can mend cars.' Usually, Chris was a romping, rolling, cheerful, round-faced, curly-haired urchin with dirty knees and a huge repertoire of noises. He spent his days being cars, spaceships, bombs, guns, jet engines and motor horns. But the bonkers clocks had changed him. His face and hair were the same as ever, but his knees were almost clean and he no longer made noises. He looked at Jenny with serious eyes. 'He can mend any car,' he said. 'Doesn't matter how bad it is, he'll mend it.'

'Bet he hasn't mended any cars today,' Dicko muttered, not wanting to get into an argument with a six-year-old.

'Course he hasn't,' Chris said. 'It's Sunday. No mending on Sunday. Sunday lunch, then fall asleep in the big armchair.' He spoke with the slow seriousness of a politician on TV. 'I sit on his lap,' Chris continued. 'Without wriggling,' he added, sternly and finally.

Jenny asked Allie, 'What are your parents doing?'

'My dear, they're being *hopeless*. Quite *hopeless*!' Allie said, looking just like her mother did when she

41

talked about her children. Even Allie's voice had the same playfully solemn tone.

'What have they been doing, actually doing?' Jenny insisted.

'*Impossible* things, dear. You'd never *believe*. *Breakfast* was quite normal but then Dad insisted on staring at the *clocks*, as if he'd never seen a clock before in his life –'

'Why was he looking at the clocks? Was there something strange about them?'

Allie looked puzzled for a moment, as if there was something she could not quite remember. The whimsical smile her mother wore when talking about the children left her face. Then she said, 'Well, I *think* there was something rather *strange* about the clocks by the time Dad had finished with them! You'll never believe – he was opening the fronts and trying to make the hands stop with his finger! Such nonsense! And then he started *being* a clock, my dear! Really, I had to laugh! There he was, wagging his head from side to side and going *tick-tock*, *tick-tock*, faster and faster! Aren't parents impossible? They get these strange ideas in their heads and there's no stopping them!'

Dicko hardly listened. He was worried: worried about the behaviour of Allie, who looked and sounded so like her mother; worried by Pete, who insisted on talking about forming a schoolchildren's union; worried by the thought of the things he should be doing to stop his and the other parents from behaving so strangely; worried most of all by the mix-up in his head – a jumble of half-remembered and half-forgotten things.

'What is your mother doing now, Allie?' Jenny said.

'Oh, she's being rather naughty. One moment it's, "Oh, do let's do some housework, I love playing house!" – and the next moment she's trying to stand on her head in the corner of the living-room, with her great feet against the wallpaper. I soon put a stop to *that*!'

'And your dad?'

'Why, my dear, I've left the pair of them in their rooms. "Enough is enough," I told them! "Either behave like sensible parents, or upstairs you go and not another word out of you until lunchtime." '

'But didn't they go to Miss Lofting's party?'

'Oh yes . . . That's right . . . They did!' Allie said, in a confused way.

'Well, don't you have to collect them and take them home and give them lunch?' Jenny said. But now she, like Dicko, was getting confused – and also impatient.

Dicko and Pete Scrivener kept talking about cars, louder and louder, with Chris interrupting . . . the words flew round in Jenny's head, blurring her mind. Cars – naughty parents – Mum and Dad driving – Ah! That was the important thing! She had to get to the police station to prevent her parents doing something silly.

'Allie – Pete – Chris – listen to me!' she said. 'We've all got to go to the police station, immediately!'

'The *police* station?' Allie said speaking in her grown-up way once again. 'Go to the police – about our own parents? Oh no, my dear. I don't *think* so. You see, Jen, I've always liked to think that I can *trust* my parents to know right from wrong. I've always felt that there must be a very special *relation-ship* within a family –'

'If the parents get into trouble,' Pete said gruffly, 'it's up to us kids to sort it out. No outside interference thank you very much.'

'They're good at *heart*,' Chris said, earnestly. 'Naughty sometimes, of course. But good at heart.' He looked very young, but sounded very old.

'Please come,' Jenny pleaded. 'Please!'

'Best left alone,' Peter said, gruffer than ever. 'Sort it out for themselves. Too much chit-chat about modern parents. Too much loose talk. All this stuff in the newspapers about delinquent parents – so much hogwash. Now, take *my* two. Nothing special about them, I don't say that; just two normal, healthy parents – bit noisy at times, bit slack about the house, I grant you that, but all the same –'

'Just what I always say!' Allie interrupted. 'I mean, what would a home be without them? Without their cheery voices, and their little hobbies? The golf clubs and food mixers and all the rest of it. Now, some people *complain* about the mess parents make. But not me. All right, I admit, sometimes Dad will get a bit peevish – trouble with his income tax, that sort of thing, *you* know how it is. Or Mum will feel a bit out of sorts because the other ladies are all wearing *this* and she's only got *that*. But, well, that's life, isn't it?'

'That's life, family life,' Pete said solemnly. 'Problems. And how do you solve those problems? I'll tell you *my* way . . .'

He told them. Dicko whispered, 'Jenny, they won't help. We've got to do it on our own.'

'Do what?' she replied, still mixed up in her head.

'The police station! We've got to go there!'

'Oh yes, of course!'

They got on their bikes and rode away, leaving Chris, Allie and Pete telling each other how they handled their parents.

The Vicar answered their knocking. However, he would not open the door of the vicarage; he knelt on the doormat behind the letterbox and shouted through it. At first, he sounded like himself – an elderly man with white hair and a trembly voice. 'Yes?' he said, 'What do you want?'

They told him, and ended by saying, 'We're sorry to disturb you.'

'I forgive you,' the Vicar said. 'I forgive everyone.'

'We're after our *parents*, not forgiveness,' Dicko said.

'Once I've forgiven you, you can't be *un*forgiven,' the Vicar said, stubbornly. 'And I've just forgiven you, so sucks boo!'

Jenny tried, 'Please, Vicar! Don't you see, we've lost our *parents* –'

' "To lose one parent may be regarded as a misfortune: to lose both looks like carelessness." I know lots more like that. Funny things to say. Clever things.'

Dicko said, 'Look: we've lost our parents. We want to find them, to get them back, is that clear?'

'What do you want them for?' said the Vicar, sounding very cunning.

'We want them because they're ours,' Dicko said.

'They're our family, we love them!' said Jenny, pathetically.

' "Children begin by loving their parents; as they grow older, they judge them; sometimes, they forgive them",' said the Vicar. 'That's jolly clever, isn't it? A clever thing to say. Ask me another question and I'll think of another answer just as clever! Go on, shout another question through the letterbox!'

'Come on, Jenny,' Dicko said. 'It's hopeless.'

They cycled on towards the police station in silence for some time, until Jenny said, 'Wait a minute. He was quoting something, wasn't he? Something from a grown-up book. Yet he was behaving like a baby as well. So how could he quote grown-up things?'

'I don't know. It's all quite mad.'

'But perhaps they're beginning to come out of the madness a little? Mr and Mrs Ramsey couldn't have quoted anything, they were too babyish, don't you remember?'

'I suppose so. I just don't know. There's the police station.'

'And there's Sergeant Wilkes. Come on!'

There was a clock over the counter in the police station. Jenny and Dicko looked at it. It was behaving normally. It showed the right time. They found Sergeant Wilkes in the back room. He was a big, red, bulging man. He generally smiled but now he was beaming. He said, 'Don't tell me – you've come to see my truncheon. And I've got handcuffs too. And a lamp that really lights.'

'We haven't come for that, Sergeant, it's about our parents.'

'It's jolly bright, my lamp! Bright as a car lamp! Brighter! Bright as brass buttons! Do you know who the king is?'

'Never mind about the king, we're trying to find our parents –'

'I'm the king! Because this is Castle Road Police Station! I'm in charge, so I'm king of the castle!' He stood on his desk, stuck his big chest out and began to sing, 'I'm the king of the castle, and you're the dirty rascal!' Jenny and Dicko just stared at him, astonished.

The Sergeant caught their eyes. He stopped singing. His smile faded. He got off the desk and burst into tears. 'You don't like me,' he said.

'We do like you,' Jenny said. 'Really we do. We like you very much. But we need your help.'

'I need help more than anyone,' the Sergeant replied. The tears rolled down his plump red cheeks. 'I've broken my brown teapot, so how can I make any tea? It's past teatime, and I want my tea.'

He cried a bit more, then said, 'Nobody likes me because I'm a policeman. They don't like policemen so they don't like *me*. But I can run people in,' he said, cheering up. 'I could run you in, if I wanted to! With my truncheon and handcuffs and all! Run you in just like that! But then,' he said, his face falling, 'if I ran you in, you wouldn't *like* me.' He began to cry again.

'At least he's talking some sense,' Dicko whispered.

'Not much,' Jenny replied. Then she said to the Sergeant, 'Just do one simple thing for us. Please. If you see our parents, tell them they must go straight home. Will you do that, Sergeant?'

'Straight home,' said the Sergeant. He was beaming again. 'Straight home, I'll tell them – and they'll obey me, because I'm the king of the castle!'

His smile faded. 'But I did tell them that,' he said. 'I told all of them that! But they wouldn't listen, however much I told them!'

'Tell whom?' Jenny said.

'Them!' said the Sergeant. 'All of them! All of them over there! All those people!'

Jenny and Dicko looked where his finger pointed.

Through the window, in the distance, they saw a mob of grown-ups.

The mob was wobbling along the street. Sometimes it stopped altogether when people began to argue, or because someone wanted to do cartwheels or try some hopscotch. In fact, the mob behaved like a kindergarten without a teacher.

Mr Finching the Bank Manager was running round the edge of the mob, sniping at Mr Rumbold. 'Pow-pow-pow! You're dead!' 'I'm not!' 'You are, I got you!' 'You didn't!' 'I did! Pow-pow-pow!'

Mr Inkpen from the garage was being a motorcycle. He made the noises with his lips and stretched out his

arms and hands to grasp imaginary handlebars. He wore his son's cowboy hat. It was too small for him.

Mrs Ramsey was still being a Dalek, and getting better at it.

Mr Scrivener was one of the few grown-ups who seemed to remember the purpose of the mob. His special Mutt Wildblood voice was getting a bit hoarse, but it still said the same things. 'Gun 'em down with our rods!' he shouted, 'by the light of the moon! Then run them outta town onna rail! D'ja get me?'

Voices answered, 'Sure thing!' and 'OK, pardner!' and even, 'You're durn tootin'!' But Mrs Rumbold, who had been doing cartwheels, suddenly stopped and stood in front of Mr Scrivener. 'Why?' she demanded.

Mr Scrivener, taken aback, said, 'Because a man's gotta do what a man's gotta do.'

'*Why?*' Mrs Rumbold said.

Mr Scrivener stuck out his lower lip and glared at Madge Rumbold. Several others of the mob gathered round to listen. Miss Lofting piped up, 'Yes! Why? Tell us why!'

Mr Scrivener said, 'Listen, sister, these Patels: they're Injuns, am I right? Right, so they're Injuns. And we gotta run them outta this territory *because* they're Injuns. Right?'

'But where they live is Injun territory,' Madge Rumbold replied, puzzled. 'I mean, their house and their shop –'

'It's them or us,' said Mr Scrivener. 'Them or us! Know what I mean, liddle sister?'

'No,' said Mrs Rumbold. 'And I'm not your little sister. I wouldn't be your little sister if you gave me a thousand pounds. And anyhow,' she continued, 'I don't know what you mean about "running them out of town on a rail". How do you do that? What sort of rail?'

Mr Scrivener felt that things were running away from him so he raised his voice to a still louder pitch. 'Listen, you guys and gals! This is white man's territory and there ain't no place, nohow, for redskins –'

'They're not red, they're brown,' Mrs Rumbold told him.

'All right, then, this ain't no place for *brown-skins* –'

'I got brown on my summer holiday,' Madge Rumbold said. 'Lovely and brown. And everyone said it looked nice. I *like* brown skins. What's *wrong* with brown skins? I spent hours and hours and days and days trying to get brown, really brown. Brown like the Patels!'

There was an uneasy silence.

Mrs Ramsey ended it by shouting, 'Well, the brownskins don't like *us*! Otherwise, they'd have come to Miss Lofting's party! But oh no, they didn't come, they were too stuck-up to come! They think they're better than us!'

Many agreed with this. There was a buzz of excited talk. Mrs Ambrose, the cake-shop lady, suddenly remembered that the Patels took the bread out of children's mouths and burst into tears. Mrs Ramsey, comforting her, cried, 'Give them an inch, and they'll take an ell!' Many people agreed with this thought, even though Mrs Rumbold said, 'What's an ell?' and no one could tell her.

One lady said, 'You won't catch me wearing soppy long dresses with gold edges!' Several others cried, 'Me neither!' 'Nor me!' 'That Mrs Patel, she's a show-off!' 'The supermarket's better than Mr Patel's rotten little shop!'

Mr Scrivener, feeling that the right moment had come, jumped up on a low wall, waved his gun over his head and shouted, 'OK, pardners! So let's get on with it, waddya say? You got guns: wadda they for?'

'Shootin'!' the men shouted.

'Who we gonna shoot?'

'The Patels!'

'When we gonna do it?'

'NOW!'

Fired with new enthusiasm, the party flashed torches, flourished guns, yelled yells and moved on with purposefully hunched shoulders, set jaws and furrowed brows. There were no more cartwheels and hopscotch; and no one to listen to Madge Rumbold, complaining, 'It's stupid! Potty! Soppy!' The voice that mattered was Mr Scrivener's when he pointed dramatically to the sky. 'Look yonder, up there, folks!'

The moon was bright in the rapidly darkening sky. 'Didn't I tell ya, folks? We're gonna gun down those pesky Patels by the light of the moon – and there's the moon, ridin' high!'

'Moon-mad,' Dicko muttered, watching the departing mob. 'Lunatics! Loonies! They could hurt someone!'

The face of the big clock caught his eye. It was not

telling the right time. Its hands were moving, faster and faster. Moving *backwards*, surely? Yet, that morning, they'd been moving *forwards*? . . .

There was no time to sort it out. The mob had to be stopped. 'Sergeant,' he said, 'those people must be brought to their senses! It's your solemn duty! You must act!'

But the Police Sergeant had caught the infection. He wanted to obey the adult, sensible voice of Dicko: but the pull of the mob was too much for him. He began to run after the crowd, shouting, 'Ah'm the law in these parts, folks, and Ah ain't standin' for no mob rule!' The mob looked at him silently. 'Leastways,' the Sergeant added, 'Ah don't *think* I am . . .' He stood there, grinning sheepishly. Mr Scrivener, seeing his uncertainty, said, 'Tell you what, Sheriff: suppose you just mosey along with us. Just to see justice done,

know what I mean? Uphold the law, kinda, like a good man should.'

'All right,' said Police Sergeant Wilkes. And went with the mob.

'We've got to stop them!' Dicko said.

'But what can we do?' Jenny asked. It was lonely watching the mob fade into the darkness: lonely and frightening. Miserably, Dicko and Jenny tailed along after the grown-ups and the lights of their torches and lanterns.

The mob was changing, slowly but surely. Mr Inkpen seemed to have realized that his son's cowboy hat looked ridiculous: he threw it into a hedge. There were no more baby voices: only grown-up voices saying silly things. But however childish the voices, the adult figures were big and menacing and the guns were real.

There was not far for the mob to go: just along the road, past the shops, round by the garage, then into the road where the village began to peter out and become countryside.

Among the last of the buildings there was a little house by a little shop, lonely in the moonlight and small against the towering trees. The sign over the shop read:

The mob stopped and was suddenly silent and serious. People spoke in hushed voices. Some said quite sensible, ordinary things, like, 'It's turning chilly', or 'I could do with a nice cup of tea.'

'Perhaps it's wearing off, whatever it is,' Jenny whispered. 'Perhaps they're getting back to normal. But I wonder what "normal" is?' Dicko did not answer. He was thinking of the clock in the police station. Its hands had been moving, moving fast. But which way? Backwards, he was sure it had been backwards.

One of the men let out a great wagon-trail whoop. 'Wha-HOO-EEEE!' Another man shouted, 'Yoicks! Tally ho!' All at once, most of the men became over-excited. They tried to dance like Red Indians, or spin their guns round their fingers like Cowboys.

Mr Blanchflower the butcher was attempting to make a hangman's noose out of a piece of electric cable.

Mr Finching was pretending he had been shot: he clutched himself and groaned, 'They got me, pardner. But tell 'em . . . I'll be . . . back . . .'

Mr Bryce, the car-hire man, was suspended by one arm from a lamp-post pretending to be a hanged man.

The wives and mothers were just as bad. Most of them were doing a sort of square-dance. Mrs Ramsey was calling out, 'Right down the middle and doh-see-doh', and clapping her hands.

'It's hopeless!' Jenny said. 'We'll never stop them now!'

57

Mr Scrivener brought the mob to order. 'OK, folks!' he shouted, quelling the din with his hoarse, high voice. 'We got a job to do. Let's do it!' And he waved his arm at the Patel house, small and silent in the moonlight.

Some of the mob cheered. Others clicked their torches on and off, or waved their guns or fingered triggers menacingly.

Then someone threw a big stone. It went through the Patels' shop window. The broken glass fell down, slivering and splintering.

Everyone was silent.

Dicko seized his chance. 'Listen, everyone!' he shouted, 'You've got to stop this! Don't you see how silly you're being?'

Jenny saw that some of the grown-ups were listening, serious-faced, to Dicko. One or two – including her own mother – even seemed anxious to leave, and ashamed and embarrassed. But then Dicko made a bad mistake. 'Go home,' he shouted, 'and stop behaving like *kids*!'

At this, there was a mumble that became a roar.

'Kids? We're not kids!'

'Who does he think he is, calling us kids?'

'I'm not a kid, I'm a grown-up. I'm *big*!'

It was Mr Finching who settled things. 'Me a *kid*?' he roared. 'I'm a Bank Manager! And jolly well grown-up! *I'm* grown-up, *you're* grown-up, we're *all* grown-ups. Well, aren't we?'

The mob roared approval.

'And we're jolly well going to duff up the Patels, aren't we?' Mr Finching appealed. 'Duff them up properly. Right?'

'Right!' the crowd roared. Guns waved and torches flared.

Then – 'Look!' Jenny said. She gripped her brother's arm.

Dicko stared into the darkness between a hedge and a shadowed wall and saw what she saw: a rounded figure with long black hair: a woman wearing a long dress of some light fabric.

The woman was attempting to skip, but the skip-ping-rope was too short for her. Hop! and jump! went the figure: but the long skirt got in the way and the head shook in grave disapproval as the woman tried again.

'Mrs Patel!' Dicko said. 'What does she think she's doing?'

'Don't you see, she's the same as the rest of them – childish –'

'She's not even looking this way!' Dicko said.

'Of course not, she's pretending not to see anyone so that people will look at her and what she's doing – and then ask if they can play too. You know the way little girls behave!'

'She wants to *play*?' Dicko said, horrified. 'Play with this lot?' The mob surged forward. Eyes flashed and teeth glinted.

And now Mr Scrivener was shouting again and waving his gun with one hand and his hat with the other. 'Injuns!' he yelled. 'Let 'em have it! C'mon, folks, let's go git that squaw!'

There was dancing and whooping and yelling. The lights of the torches were like fireworks. The mob was like a big untidy animal with too many limbs, thrash-ing itself forward. 'Yippee!' this big animal shouted. 'Let's go!'

The shadowy figure of Mrs Patel solemnly bent to straighten the skipping-rope. Her head was still coyly turned away from the mob. Yet again, she tried little girlish hops over the rope and yet again it tangled itself in her long skirt. Dicko groaned.

Mr Ramsey, frantic-faced, was yelling louder than anyone and at the same time, tugging at the safety catch of his pistol. It flashed in his hands. 'Yow-EEE!' he screamed – pulled the trigger – and the blank cartridge exploded with a great flash and an astonishingly loud bang, so loud that there had to be a silence after the explosion.

In the quietness, Dicko and Jenny saw Mr Ramsey's face. The mouth was a black O of surprise. As they watched, Mr Ramsey slid slowly to the ground. He sat there, holding his left leg with both hands.

'Oh, my foot!' he cried. 'My poor foot!'

He started to cry, noisily.

The front door of the Patel house opened and two children came out: Dipika and her brother Radi. He was eleven, she was almost nine. Dipika went to her mother and tried to pull her into the house, but her mother didn't want to come.

Radi strode briskly down the path from the house. People moved aside to let him through. 'All right,' Radi said. 'Someone tell me what's been happening.'

His mother skipped to his side and said, 'There was a bang! So loud! I heard the bang, I was skipping and there was a big bang!'

Radi took no notice of the little-girl voice. 'What happened?' he demanded. 'What do all you people think you're doing? Come on, now! The truth!'

Mr Scrivener said, 'We'd come to git you. We wuz gonna run you outta town onna rail . . .' His voice sounded uncertain. His head dropped.

Mr Rumbold said, 'You see, this is Injun territory because you're an Injun. Indian, I mean. So we thought we'd come here and . . . sort of run you out of town on a rail,' he ended unhappily. Even his Wild West accent had let him down.

Mr Ramsey said, 'My foot! My foot! It hurts!' He was still crying.

Mr Scrivener began to cry too. Mrs Patel, suddenly looking older, put her arm round his shoulders and said, 'Don't be upset. I'm sure you didn't mean any harm. I'm sure it wasn't your fault.' But now Mr Scrivener really was crying. 'It *was* my fault!' he said.

'All my fault! It was that stupid game, I made them play it, it was my fault!'

Radi and some of the men took Mr Ramsey into the house. Mrs Patel knelt by the sofa on which he lay, patting his hand while Mr Ramsey's wounded foot was stripped of its shoe and sock and inspected.

'Broken glass!' someone said. 'I thought he'd shot himself with that gun of his!'

'No, he must have stepped on a broken bottle or something.'

'It's gone right through his shoe!'

'And right into his foot!'

'I bet it hurts like mad!'

'It *still* hurts!' Mr Ramsey said, proudly. 'It's agony! And look at all my blood!'

The room became crowded with people, most of them standing about uselessly. Dipika was busy getting bandages and a clean rag. Radi was in the kitchen boiling a big saucepan of water. He had the bottle of disinfectant ready and was preparing to bathe the wound.

The men were embarrassed and mumbled about the dangers of broken glass. But the women broke the ice. Mrs Inkpen said to Mrs Patel, 'I say, I do like your house! You've got lovely things!' She pointed at the pictures and ornaments. 'Brilliant!' smiled Mrs Inkpen, pointing at a line of little elephants made of ebony, crossing a wooden bridge, 'Fantastic! The elephants get smaller and smaller, smaller and smaller. And they've got nice little round eyes! Terrific!'

Mrs Patel smiled and wriggled with pleasure. She said, 'And see this picture! It is made from butterfly wings, the wings of real butterflies! The biggest butterflies you have ever seen!'

Mrs Ramsey said, 'My auntie had a picture just like that. It was made of wings, just the same.' She sniffed haughtily.

'Bet she didn't!' Mrs Patel said.

'Oh yes she did. Butterfly wings, just the same.'

'Bet it wasn't,' said Mrs Patel.

'No, it wasn't,' said Mrs Ramsey, nastily. 'It was better!'

'Bet it wasn't, Mrs Patel said.

'The wings were bigger,' said Mrs Ramsey.

'Bet they weren't.'

The two women glowered at each other. Jenny watched them both, wondering about them, and herself, and everyone. She felt herself changing, very slightly and slowly, back to her real self. Or did she? But here were two grown-up women behaving like silly children. Would they change? When? This, year, next year, some time, never? Certainly Mrs Ramsey's expression was changing . . .

'Perhaps,' Mrs Ramsey said, her face softening, 'Perhaps your butterfly picture is nicer than my auntie's. And I like your curtains. And I think your dress is pretty.'

Mrs Patel smiled shyly. Mrs Ramsey smiled back. 'Then we can be friends,' said Mrs Patel.

'Thank goodness for that,' thought Jenny.

Now that the shoe was cut away and the wound cleaned and washed, you could see what had happened to Mr Ramsey's foot. The glass had made quite an ugly little cut in the edge of it. 'It's not so bad after all,' said Radi.

'It feels bad,' Mr Ramsey said, 'It feels *awful*. Oooo!'

'No bones broken,' Radi said, ignoring Mr Ramsey's appealing look. 'You've been lucky this time, my lad,' he added. Then, addressing everyone, he said, 'But no more dropping glass bottles around, right?'

'Right,' everyone agreed, humbly.

'And no more fooling about with guns, either,' Radi said sternly.

'No more guns,' said Mr Ramsey humbly.

'Promise, now?'

'Promise,' muttered Mr Ramsey. Now his face was pink with shame. He did not make a sound when Dipika put disinfectant and a plaster on the wound, though it must have hurt a bit; he just bit his lips and stared trustingly into her eyes. She told him he was a

65

brave little chap, a proper little soldier. As a reward she gave him a biscuit with red jelly in the middle. Mr Ramsey munched it and began to smile.

But then Mr Patel entered the room. He was in a very bad temper. He stamped his foot on the floor and shouted, 'You are very bad people, you have broken my shop window all to pieces!' He did not speak English as well as his children.

Nobody had remembered about breaking Mr Patel's shop window. Until he came in, everyone had been quite happy. It was rather as if a party were starting. All the grown-ups were chattering and Mrs Patel handed out sweet biscuits. Some of the men were even beginning to wrestle with each other, but very carefully, so as not to damage the furniture in the little room. Mr Patel was so angry that the jollity had to stop.

'Yes, my window is broken all to pieces!' he cried. Everyone looked at the floor. There were murmurs of 'It wasn't me!' and '*He* did it.' Someone even said, 'Broken window, what a fuss!' but this remark caused scandalized Ssshes. Everybody was upset because Mr Patel was so upset.

It was Mr Scrivener who said, 'I think it was stupid, busting Mr Patel's window. They're expensive, those windows, they cost pounds and pounds and now we've gone and bust it.'

Mr Inkpen said, 'We were only playing, it wasn't really our fault, we didn't mean it. Anyhow, it's bound to be insured!'

Mr Patel said, sadly, 'It was not insured. I do not have money for such things as insuring windows.' A tear rolled down his cheek. 'It was all your faults,' he said, bitterly.

Mr Scrivener said, 'He's right. It was our fault, and we've got to do something about it! And if you won't, I will!'

Red-faced, he plunged his hands into his pockets and started throwing all the money he could find on to a sofa cushion. He had plenty of silver and a five pound note in his wallet. He put all the money on the cushion.

Someone began to clap and then they were all clapping and looking for money. Very soon there was a big pile of money on the sofa and Mr Patel was saying, 'No more! No more! That is enough! Too much!' He ran from person to person, trying to thrust money into pockets and purses and wallets, but as soon as he succeeded in returning someone's money, that person laughed and threw it back on the pile.

In the end, Mr Patel sat on a chair, buried his face in his hands and burst into tears. It was Mr Inkpen who said, 'Why are you crying, Mr Patel? What have we done wrong?'

Mr Patel said, 'You are very kind, that is all. I did not think you were kind but you are. And besides, that is too much money for a window. It is only a little store with a little window.'

He stood up, his face wet with tears. Everyone looked at him anxiously. Then suddenly he started laughing. 'It is nice, nice!' he cried. 'You are very nice people! I have more biscuits, lots of them, and good tea! And jam, and little cakes!'

He pushed his wife towards the kitchen to get the food. Now everyone was laughing, even Mr Ramsey, whose foot was tidily bound up. He hopped about on his good foot, saying, 'Yes, cakes! Let's all eat cakes and have a dance, or something. That is, if Mrs Patel doesn't mind.' Mrs Patel beamed at him but Dipika told him to sit down quietly, 'You've had quite enough excitement for one day,' she said.

Nevertheless, the party went on long after all the cakes and biscuits had been eaten.

It was such an enjoyable party that no one seemed to notice what the clock on the Patels' mantelpiece was doing. Its hands were whizzing round, but not quite so fast.

It struck all the hours when there were still plenty of cakes and biscuits left.

It went through them all again when there was nothing left to eat and drink and people were wondering what to do with their empty plates. Not that empty plates mattered much. Everyone was having a good time. Yet the party was changing.

Dicko said, 'Have you noticed, Jen? They've stopped playing rough games. They're not belting up and down the stairs yelling their heads off. They're getting quieter.'

'Perhaps they're just getting tired,' Jen said.

'No, look at them! They're not behaving like kids any more. They're like grown-ups.'

Jen said, 'Pity in a way. I'm feeling all lively. I'd like to do something energetic. Something *stupid*. Toboggan down the stairs on a tea tray, something like that. Look, there's a tea tray over there . . .'

'Well you can't,' Dicko said. 'It's not that sort of party any more. I mean, just look at them! Our parents and everyone!'

She looked. Her brother was right. The Bank Manager was saying to Mr Patel, 'The banks are bulging with money at the moment. Anyone who wants a loan to extend his business – a business like yours, for example – should see to it now, while the money's still there for the asking. Of course, I'm not presuming to advise you, but if you ever want to call in and have a chat –'

'A chat,' said Mr Patel. 'Yes, I would like that.'

'And look,' Dicko said, 'at Mr Scrivener!' He was joining in the conversation between Mr Ramsey and Mr Patel. 'That window of yours,' he said. 'I'm in the tool-hire business and I've got a friend who's in the glass line. Now, if I got him to deliver the glass – I'd measure it all up, of course, and me and some lads I know would put it in for you . . .'

'They're getting back to normal!' Jenny said. 'They're growing up again! Look at Mrs Ramsey!'

Mrs Ramsey was talking about the urgent need for

70

a proper school crossing. 'The cars come roaring round Elm Road corner, it's not right!'

'We parents must get together and persuade the council,' Mrs Inkpen said. 'If enough of us act – you'd sign a sort of petition, wouldn't you, Mrs Patel?'

'Of course I would!' said Mrs Patel. You could see how pleased she was to have been asked: how happy it made her to be part of the village, instead of a foreigner living in 'Injun territory'.

Miss Lofting appeared at the doorway and was greeted by the Patels. Miss Lofting was her usual self, polite, cautious and quiet. But there was a slight chilly edge to her voice when she said to Mrs Patel, 'I'm *so* sorry you could not attend my little party this morning. I had hoped that *all* the parents would come.'

'But how could I?' Mrs Patel answered, her eyes wide with surprise. 'Dipika has a *rash*, only a little one, but you never know, it might be infectious – all the children in the school might catch it! But you know this, I sent a note to you to explain!'

'Oh!' said Miss Lofting. Her face changed. Now it was she who had to explain. 'Oh, of course! I saw the note, I held it in my hand, but – this is most unlike me! – I never opened it, I was so busy getting things ready for my little gathering . . .'

'And besides,' she added, 'it has been such a strange day . . .'

The clock went *Ping*. Nine o'clock.

Its hands moved very slowly, no longer racing through the minutes and hours.

All at once, it seemed time to go, time to finish the party.

'I had no idea it was so late!' said Mrs Ramsey. 'Mrs Patel, what must you think of us? Invading your house, staying so late . . . But we have enjoyed ourselves so much!'

'So have we,' said Mrs Patel. 'Very, very much.'

Everyone moved to the front door. Once there, half in and half out of the house, the party seemed briefly to revive itself and linger on. Dicko and Jenny stood silently, listening and watching. A woman who had been a nurse was saying, 'But Mrs Patel, I've looked at Dipika, I hope you don't mind, and I assure you that that's not a *measles* rash and it's not a *scarlet-fever* rash. It's just a *rash*.'

Mr Scrivener was saying, 'First thing tomorrow morning, then, right? Me and the lads. Fix up that window in a jiffy. One of Sergeant Wilkes' men will keep an eye on the shop front during the night, right, Sergeant?' The Police Sergeant said, 'Aye,' and shook Mr Patel's hand solemnly, beaming at him in his old, fatherly, policemanly way.

As for Dipika and Radi – they were behaving just like children, running round searching for any sweet biscuits that might have been left and trying to walk on their hands when they didn't find any. Dipika could do it, Radi could not. 'Anyone can do it!' he puffed, falling over his own head. 'It's potty!' he said, falling over the other way.

Dicko and Jenny smiled at each other and started walking homewards. They too felt different. Or was it that they merely felt cheerful and relieved? 'Back to normal,' Dicko said.

'And very nice too,' Jenny said.

The dew was heavy in the long grass. Dicko tried to kick the cold drops on to Jenny. She screamed and splashed dew at him with her hands. They did not notice various guns lying, like forgotten toys, in the dewy grass and on the road in front of the Patels' house. Next day, Mr Scrivener found them and, without a word, gathered them up, threw them in the back of his van and dumped them in the duckpond.

Exactly at bedtime, when all the older children were being chivvied upstairs and not being allowed to watch TV a moment longer; and all the young children were asleep, with one arm thrown across their teddy bears; and all the grown-ups were yawning the first yawn of late evening and remembering that tomorrow was Monday and back to work, oh dear me; exactly at this time, every clock in every house resumed its usual habit of telling the proper time and going at the proper rate.

Stanley the cat, tired, ruffled and grumpy after his kittenish day, kneaded a cushion with his front paws and poked a suspicious nose into the hollow he had made. Then, very carefully, he settled himself into the hollow, tucked his head into his shoulders, and began to purr himself to sleep.

Jenny and Dicko whispered (which they were forbidden to do, but always did) across the hall separating their bedrooms. 'That bloke Radi has got the same computer as mine, but all sorts of different programmes. We're going to do swaps, it'll be great . . .'

Jenny said, 'Dipika has got photos of two of my favourite pop stars – and they're actually *signed*! I just *hate* her – except I don't really, of course, she's great.'

Mrs Rumbold said, 'This tea's awful. It's stewed. What a peculiar day, I've never known one like it!'

'Don't know what you mean,' said Mr Rumbold, rustling the paper he wanted to read. 'It was just another Sunday. Except for Miss Lofting's party, of course. And meeting the Patels. Nice people.'

'No, there *was* something funny about today,' said Mrs Rumbold. 'But I can't remember what. Was it some sort of game we played?'

'Oh, that reminds me – Mr Patel and I are playing tennis next Saturday,' said her husband. 'Need the exercise.' He turned on the TV.

The screen lit up. Cowboys and Indians. 'Ya know what?' said a tough-looking cowboy. 'We're goin' to run you coyotes outta town. Onna rail!' Mr Rumbold made a face and turned the set off. 'Childish drivel,' he grumbled. 'Can't imagine who watches that sort of stuff.'

They sat doing nothing in particular, very comfortably. Above their heads, the clock on the mantelpiece ticked in its usual quiet way, at its usual rate. 'Three minutes fast,' said Mr Rumbold, as he gave the clock its weekly wind. 'Three minutes fast, as usual.' He patted the clock on the head, then closed its glass carefully.

All through the village, people said, 'Just look at the time! Monday tomorrow . . . Suppose we'd better turn in.'

By the time all the clocks in the village agreed it was midnight, only a few lights showed from the houses. Then they too went out, and the world was left to bats and cats, owls and foxes, badgers and mice; while the faithful clocks ticked away the night.